CONTENTS

ISBN 0-8497-9324-6

About the author

Beth Gigante has been an independent piano teacher since 1967. Her current studio is in her home in Alexandria, Virginia, where she is an active member of many music teachers' organizations. She has given presentations to music teacher groups on studio organization and business policies across the country.

Ms. Gigante has played piano, harp, and viola in various orchestra, chamber, and solo performances. Her Bachelor's degree in Piano Performance was from Syracuse University; her Master's degree in Piano Performance was granted by the University of Michigan.

PREFACE

One of the most important aspects of running a successful private studio is maintaining a professional attitude. It is important that we have a feeling of pride in what we do and that we project that pride to others. A well-organized, business-like, professional studio projects this. Our musical knowledge and skills are the most important assets of our profession, but our business skills, or lack of them, affect that profession.

I feel strongly that the business must run smoothly if the music is to flow. As an independent music teacher, I take great pride in what I do. I am proud to be a musician, to be a teacher, and to be self-employed and operating a successful studio.

Having lectured extensively throughout the United States, one of my main professional goals has been to address the issue of the business aspects of private music teaching. In order to project a professional image and to earn a salary worthy of our training, all independent music teachers must educate themselves in this area.

As in any business, organization is essential for a smoothly-run studio. If a teacher's business runs smoothly—payments come on time, make-up policy is respected, a clear bookkeeping system is in order, and appropriate salary is enjoyed—there is much greater chance that the teaching will also run smoothly.

This book is a summary of my research in this area, and is meant as a practical business guide for the independent music teacher. Musical matters are not addressed here, nor are any concepts on teaching. Instead, this book is intended to reflect what I have learned, during the course of my teaching and my travels, about the most efficient and workable studio policies. Please take these ideas as suggestions on which to build your own personal policies.

Our profession is one which deserves great respect, and it is up to us to initiate that respect.

My thanks to my sister, DonnaMarie Honsinger for her invaluable suggestions and her hours of help to make this book a reality. Many thanks also to my husband, Kal Klingenstein, for his support and good common sense.

Beth Gigante

CHAPTER 1

THE STUDENT INTERVIEW

Before accepting a new or transfer student, interview the student and the parents to be sure there can be a good rapport and that the student has some potential. There are no guarantees, of course, but an interview can help eliminate surprises on either side.

Interview the student first and then interview the parents. Just a few of the questions you might wish to ask a beginning student are:

- Why are you taking music lessons?
- Have you ever played a music instrument?
- Have you had music classes in school?
- Does anyone in your family play a music instrument?
- What other activities do you have after school?
- How much time do you think you will be practicing?

When the transfer student comes for the interview, have him or her perform a few pieces. (This request should be made when the interview appointment is made.) Have him sight-read, clap some written rhythms, and ask some theory questions. Try to find out what kind of student he is; what habits he has.

The interview of the transfer student is very important. If a student says he has been studying for five years (and plays on a first-year level); he has had six teachers in that time; he is taking music lessons because of parental pressure; and he does not practice because he hates it, you may wish to consider the factors strongly.

A few of the questions you might ask a student who has had previous lessons are:

- How long have you been playing the (violin, piano, flute, etc.)?
- How many teachers have you studied with?
- Why are you changing teachers?
- What performance experience do you have?
- Who is your favorite composer?
- What is your favorite piece of music?
- How much do you practice?
- What other activities do you have after school?

When interviewing the parents, try to get a feeling about the support they will be offering to their child. Find out if they play an instrument, what their work schedules are, and what the student's outside activities are (student and parent versions may vary). Review every item on the policy sheet with the parents and make sure they have a copy when they leave the interview.

CHAPTER 2

THE POLICY SHEET

When interviewing a prospective student and parent(s), have a *written* studio policy sheet to give to the parent(s) *after reviewing it* with them. The policy sheet should include topics such as:

- Fees for lessons.
- Payment procedures for lessons.
- Calendar for the year, including the schedule for group lessons if appropriate.
- Policy on missed lessons.
- Expectations for recitals, festivals, and workshops.
- Policy on summer lessons/payments.
- Miscellaneous items such as
    - how to keep a well-maintained instrument
    - appropriate time of day for phone calls
    - short fingernails or other physical requirements
    - parental attendance at lessons.

The interview is the time to make your business policies clear. If the student and parents agree to start lessons with you after being informed of your studio business policies, they are obligated to follow those policies. To avoid future confusion, make sure that all policies are clear and that the student and parents leave with a written copy of your policies. By maintaining a professional manner, let it be known that this is your business.

The following example of a policy sheet shows ways in which certain items may be covered. Teachers should adjust items to their individual circumstances.

Mrs. Kathleen Jones•24 Main Street•Hometown, VA 12345
555-2222•mrsjones@hometown.net

POLICY SHEET FOR 20--

Please save this for reference!

CALENDAR

Lessons will begin on September 4, 20--. No lessons will be taught on the following days:

October 13	**Columbus Day**
November 21-23	**Thanksgiving Holiday**
December 24-January 2	**Winter Holiday**
One week in Spring (TBA)	**Spring Holiday**
One week in Summer (TBA)	**Summer Holiday**

Regular lessons will be taught on all other school holidays.

TUITION

The year will be divided into three semesters. Tuition is due the first lesson of each semester, and encompasses recitals, workshops, theory classes, and lessons.

September 4-January 11	$________	45-minute lessons
	$________	60-minute lessons
January 14-May 31	$________	45-minute lessons
	$________	60-minute lessons
June 3-August 3	To be announced	

Payment towards tuition may also be made in monthly installments. These payments are due in advance on the first lesson of each month. Monthly tuition remains constant regardless of the number of lessons received in any given month.

45-minute lessons	$________	monthly installments
60-minute lessons	$________	monthly installments

OVERDUE TUITION FEE

If a monthly installment is not received by the 15th of the month, a $5.00 overdue fee will be added.

MISSED LESSONS

Make-up lessons will only be given when 24-hour notice is given for sickness, or if sudden extreme weather conditions occur. Make-ups will not be given for any other reason.

If you wish, you can have your name, phone number, and lesson time published on a "lesson swap" list. All students who choose to be on the swap list will receive a copy and can then rearrange lessons for important and unavoidable conflicts. (Students whose names are not on the swap list will not receive a copy.) I must be notified in advance of changed lesson times.

If a student cannot attend the lesson for reasons other than those listed above and cannot arrange a swap, the lesson is forfeited. If the teacher cannot attend a lesson for reasons other than those listed above, and cannot arrange a swap, the teacher will forfeit the income.

BOOK DEPOSIT

All students are required to make a $30.00 book deposit at the beginning of the September semester. A record will be kept of all book expenses and other miscellaneous fees. When the $30.00 is depleted, a copy of the expense record will be given to the parents and another $30.00 will be deposited. If the student should terminate lessons, any unused deposit will be refunded.

GROUP ACTIVITIES

A yearly calendar will be given to each student with the dates of all the group activities. Students are expected to attend all group functions. Tuition will not be altered in any way should a student be unable to attend group activities.

Group theory classes will be held on Saturdays. Students are expected to check their calendars for dates. There will be approximately two theory classes a month for each student.

Group performance workshops will be held on Sunday afternoons approximately once a month. Check the calendar for all dates.

PERFORMANCES

There will be two recitals, one in December and one in May, with rehearsals held in advance.

Students should take advantage of performing opportunities in all workshops, recitals, festivals, and competitions for which the teacher, student, and parents feel he is prepared.

SUMMER SEMESTER

Students are expected to continue lessons through the summer. Summer tuition may be prorated only when the student is on vacation out of town. If a student is in town and chooses not to take lessons in the summer, there will be no guarantee of a fall lesson time.

MISCELLANEOUS

All students are required to have a well-maintained instrument, a metronome, and a music dictionary.

All students must have short fingernails. Fingernails should be cut as short as possible, flush with the end of the finger. Students who arrive for their lesson with long fingernails will either use lesson time to cut their nails, or will be sent home.

Please park on the road adjacent to my house. The road in front of the other houses should not be used for parking.

Please be sure your child is inside my house before driving away!

Parents are not invited inside the studio during lessons.

If you have questions or concerns, please call between 9:30 a.m. and 10:30 p.m.

Let's all look forward to an exciting year of learning!

CHAPTER 3

TUITION & MAKE-UPS

When setting the tuition you must consider the "market" in your area. Many different aspects of your geographical area must be considered. Some points to consider are:

- How much are other teachers in the area charging?
- Is there a shortage of teachers or students?
- What is usually offered by other studios?
- What could make your studio special?
- Are you more (or less!) educated/experienced than most teachers in the area, and how will that affect your rate structure?

You may find answers to these questions through chatting with members of the local music teachers' organization at a meeting, or through a formal survey of members of the same, or similar, organization. See page 32 for an example of such a survey.

RAISING TUITION

It is best to raise tuition at regular intervals. When raising the tuition, consider that year's inflation. If inflation has gone up 5%, you must raise your rates 5% in order to make the same salary you made the previous year. If you feel that you deserve a raise, you must increase your salary by more than the rate of inflation. June is a good time to raise rates.

Music teachers have traditionally had low salaries. Keep in mind that *we set our own salaries*. With our training, and the amount of work that we do outside of lesson time, we deserve an acceptable salary! Besides the time given to lessons and preparation, we review repertoire, attend workshops and festivals, and practice. We must also consider that we do not receive benefits in addition to our salary: there is no sick leave, paid vacations, company retirement fund, medical insurance, paid holidays, paid personal leave, or disability insurance. Our rates must encompass the cost of all these concerns.

When informing parents of an increase in rates, do so in a professional manner. Send a letter for this purpose only, and be brief. There is no need to justify, explain, or defend an increase in rates. An example of a rate increase notice is given.

Rate Increase Notice Example

Mrs. Kathleen Jones•24 Main Street•Hometown, VA 12345
555-2222•mrsjones@hometown.net

April 20, 20--

Dear Parents and Students:
As of June 1, 20--, my rates will be:
$_________ a month for 45-minute lessons; $_________ per semester.
$_________ a month for 60-minute lessons; $_________ per semester.

Sincerely,

Kathleen Jones

INVOICING FOR BOOKS

When billing for books, you can either ask for a book deposit or bill for books on a monthly basis. Students and parents can be made responsible for getting their own books, but some teachers prefer to buy for the students so that they will be certain the correct music is available on time.

A book deposit fee can eliminate monthly fluctuation in payments. Each teacher can assess the amount of the deposit based on personal criteria. When using a deposit method, keep a record of each student's account. When the deposit is depleted, send a copy of the student's record and ask for another deposit. An example of a book deposit record is shown.

Book Deposit Record Example

BOOK DEPOSIT RECORD

for *Susan Smith*

Date	Item	Credit +	Debit -	Balance
9/7	Book Deposit	30.00		30.00
9/21	Chopin Nocturnes		7.95	22.05
10/5	Debussy La Cathedrale . . .		2.95	19.10
11/7	Bartok Mikrokosmos Bk. VI		3.50	15.60
12/15	Haydn Sonatas Vol. III		13.50	2.10
BOOK DEPOSIT DUE				
1/1	Book Deposit	30.00		32.10

If monthly billing for books is preferred, send a written statement at the end of the month covering all books and fees for that month. Be sure to keep a copy for your files. An example is given.

Monthly Book Invoice Example

MONTHLY BOOK INVOICE

Date *October 30* 20____

Name *Susan Smith*

1			
2	*Beethoven Sonatas*	*15*	*00*
3			
4	*Bartok Mik. Bk. VI*	*3*	*50*
5			
6			
7	*total due:*	*18*	*50*
8			
9			
10			
11			
12			
13			
14			
15			

OVERDUE NOTICES

It is advisable to send a written statement if payment is overdue, rather than have a direct conversation on the subject. A conversation can result in a justification on why payment is late and a debate on who needs the money more might follow. A short written "overdue bill" (an example is given) results in a quicker response and is more professional. It is fair for you to add a late-payment fee of either a set amount, or a percentage of the total amount overdue. Enclosing a self-addressed envelope often results in a more prompt payment.

Overdue Notice Example

OVERDUE NOTICE

Date July 15 20____

Name Susan Smith

1			
2	Amt. Due 7/1	80	00
3			
4	Overdue Fee	5	00
5			
6			
7	Total due	85	00
8			
9			
10			
11			
12			
13			
14			
15			

INVOICING FOR LESSONS

When billing for lessons, there are three possible methods from which to choose: **weekly, monthly, or semester** payment. Weekly payments provide the most problems. If a student misses a lesson, he is not there to pay for that week's lesson. It is very difficult to maintain a steady income with weekly payments. It is also close to impossible to budget when money "trickles in" in small amounts.

A system of **monthly** payments is more efficient. It is also helpful to use the term "tuition" instead of "monthly lesson cost." To arrive at a charge for tuition, consider that when holidays are subtracted from the months between September to May, 36 weeks are left, providing an average of four lessons a month over the nine months. Tuition covers not only lessons, but other activities as well. The payments remain constant. This is beneficial to the parent, who knows that the same amount is always due on the first of the month; and for the teacher, who knows exactly how much income will be there on the first of the month. The summer months usually have to be prorated due to extended vacations.

A **semester** payment schedule is also very efficient. The year can be divided into three semesters: September to mid-January; mid-January to May; and the summer. The first two semesters can have 18 lessons each, with the tuition based on that number of lessons. Tuition for the summer months should be made payable at the beginning of the summer. Some teachers offer 34 (instead of 36) lessons over a nine-month period to provide a two-weeks paid vacation. This can be achieved just by stating on the policy sheet calendar which weeks will not have lessons.

LENGTH OF LESSONS

If you decide to change from 30 minute lessons to 45 minutes (or any other time period), it's best not to raise rates at the same time. An increase in tuition (because of longer lesson times) will automatically be felt by parents, and it is best not to add to that with a rate increase. When you decide to change the length of lessons, simply send out a notice stating that all lessons are being changed to a specified length, based on the same rate structure used in the past, but providing greater opportunities for growth in each student.

THE SWAP LIST

Teachers should not be expected to accommodate each student when there is a last-minute need or desire to change a lesson time. A Lesson Swap List provides a good solution for teachers and students. By providing a list of the students' names, phone numbers, and lesson times, students can rearrange their own lesson when a problem occurs. (An example is given.) The teacher is to be notified of the swap. Only students who wish to be on the list will have their phone numbers included, and only those students on the list will receive a copy of it. Names of students who are not interested in swapping are listed with no phone number, to prevent parents from saying "I see you have a vacant slot at . . . ." The opportunity to be on the list should be explained in the interview and on the policy sheet.

Lesson Swap List Example

LESSON SWAP LIST

Phone numbers are given for those interested in swapping.

MONDAY

2:15-3	Carol Turner	555-9876
3-3:45	Bruce Johnston*	555-2233
3:45-4:30	Diana Rogers	555-4311
6:15-7	(David Lopez)	
7-7:45	(Jan Fenner)	
7:45-8:30	Lydia Shen	555-3456
8:30-9:15	Victor Quezada	555-6161

*Adult Student

TUESDAY

3:15-4	Andrew Neeley	555-0033
4-4:45	Janice Strobl	555-4567

(to be completed for all lesson times)

MAKE-UP LESSONS

To avoid the distress of make-up lessons, have a firm policy to present in the interview and repeat it on the policy sheet. Parents (or adult students) are much more respectful of the situation when there is a clear rule to follow.

As discussed in the preceding paragraphs, the Swap List is a wonderful aid to avoid make-up lessons, but it does not really cover situations such as weather conditions or illness. Some teachers may feel more comfortable establishing a policy that covers certain cancellations that MAY be made up, explaining them at the interview and on the policy sheet. Other teachers may feel that it is not necessary to offer make-ups for any reason. Whatever the policy is, be sure to state it clearly and to be consistent in its enforcement.

CHAPTER 4

GROUP LESSONS

Group lessons can be used to teach theory, to provide performance classes, to supplement private lessons, or to replace private lessons. The group lesson can bring many extra benefits to both student and teacher, but they also bring extra challenges in billing and scheduling to the teacher.

When teachers offer group lessons, they are offering more services to the student and can therefore increase the tuition. The overall tuition should be increased to reflect the increase in services the student is receiving. This also offers the benefit of increased income to the teacher. More importantly, this avoids the problem of students and/or parents making "a la carte menu" selections and deciding not to take (or pay for) a portion of their musical education that the teacher believes is crucial to the overall study of music.

One word of caution: Be sure that you are aware of local zoning laws before you teach group lessons. Some zoning laws limit the number of students you can teach at one time in your home. Other laws limit the total number of students you can teach in a day in your home. If this is true, you may need to find another location to teach your group lessons such as a church, school, or commercial studio.

GROUP LESSONS IN ADDITION TO PRIVATE LESSONS

Many teachers offer lessons in combination with private lessons. One possibility is to teach four private lessons a month and one or two group lessons a month.

Scheduling the private lessons would be the same as mentioned earlier. A suggested schedule for two group lessons a month is:

Tuesday	Sept. 7	Sept. 14	Sept. 21	Sept. 28
7:00-8:00 p.m.	Group 1	Group 3	Group 1	Group 3
8:00-9:00 p.m.	Group 2	Group 4 & above	Group 2	Group 4 & above

Some teachers base tuition for group lessons at one-half the hourly rate for private lessons. Tuition is charged whether the student attends the class or not.

If a teacher had 30 private students and they each came for group lessons once a month, the teacher would receive the same income as if she had taught 15 private lessons. This could be accomplished in two to four hours, depending on the number of groups taught. Two group lessons a month per student would be the same as receiving income from an entire week of private teaching and could be accomplished in as little as four to eight hours of teaching.

THEORY CLASSES

Teaching theory can often be most productive for both student and teacher when students are taught in groups. The chance of not covering a specific item is less in a class than in a private lesson. Theory classes can be offered one or two times a month, in addition to private lessons.

An example of scheduling each student in a class two times a month is:

Saturday	Sept. 4	Sept. 11	Sept. 18	Sept. 25
10:00-11:15 a.m.	Level 1	Levels 3-4	Level 1	Levels 3-4
11:15-12:30 p.m.	Level 2	Level 5 & above	Level 2	Level 5 & above

Tuition can be arranged in one of two ways. The charge for theory classes can be included in the overall tuition amount, or, if the teacher prefers to have an independent charge for theory classes, it should be a policy that payments are expected even when the student does not attend classes.

PERFORMANCE CLASSES

By performing for their peers on a regular basis, students can rid themselves of a great deal of stage fright. When parents and other "outsiders" are not present, performing in front of a group that becomes a group of friends is a challenge—but a friendly challenge. Performance classes held one or two times a month can offer the experience needed to make recitals, festivals, and competitions more relaxed.

An example of scheduling performance classes with students of similar abilities once a month is given:

Sunday, Sept. 29	1:00-2:00	Beginner
	2:00-3:00	Intermediate
	3:00-4:00	Advanced
Sunday, Oct. 26	1:00-2:00	Beginner
	2:00-3:00	Intermediate
	3:00-4:00	Advanced

Levels could also be mixed within each hour to expose the students to all levels of playing. The students could be divided into Groups A, B, and C and scheduled accordingly.

The payment can be made much the same as with theory classes—either increase the overall tuition, or add on an additional, non-refundable fee for performance class.

GROUP LESSONS AS THE ONLY LESSONS

Some teachers prefer to give all lessons in groups (no private lessons at all), feeling that students benefit from always working with their peers. In addition, the teacher can decrease teaching time without decreasing income. Group lessons can be offered from one to four times a week, depending on the student and teacher requirements.

An example of scheduling two group lessons a week is given:

Group A	4 students	Group F	4 students
Group B	3 students	Group G	3 students
Group C	4 students	Group H	2 students
Group D	2 students	Group I	4 students
Group E	4 students		

	Mon.	Tues.	Wed.	Thurs.	Fri.
3:30-4:30 p.m.	A	B	A	B	H
4:30-5:30 p.m.	C	E	C	E	I
5:30-6:30 p.m.	I	F	D	F	D
6:30-7:30 p.m.	G	H	G	—	—

The schedule given provides the following:

- 30 students receive two 60-minute lessons a week.
- Each student pays the same as a private 60-minute lesson, but receives two 60-minute lessons.
- The teacher earns income equal to 30 hours of private teaching in 18 hours of group teaching.

COMING EVENTS SCHEDULING

It is very easy for a parent or student to forget a scheduled event. To avoid this, the teacher should prepare a calendar of coming events, including the date, time, event, location, and attendees expected. Ask parents to keep the schedule for reference.

After the letter has been duplicated, write the family name on each one. That way, if a copy is left behind in the studio, you will know whose copy it is.

EXAMPLE 1

Mrs. Kathleen Jones•24 Main Street•Hometown, VA 12345
555-2222•mrsjones@hometown.net

September 2, 20--

COMING EVENTS CALENDAR FOR THEORY & PERFORMANCE CLASSES.

Please mark these dates on your calendar!
Save this copy for reference.

Saturday	Sept. 14	10:00-11:15	Level 1	Theory Class
		11:30-12:45	Level 2	Theory Class
Saturday	Sept. 21	10:00-11:15	Levels 3-4	Theory Class
		11:30-12:45	Levels 5-6	Theory Class
Saturday	Sept. 28	10:00-11:15	Level 1	Theory Class
		11:30-12:45	Level 2	Theory Class
Sunday	Sept. 29	1:00-2:00	Beginning	Performance Class
		2:00-3:00	Intermediate	Performance Class
		3:00-4:00	Advanced	Performance Class
Saturday	Oct. 5	10:00-11:15	Levels 3-4	Theory Class
		11:30-12:45	Levels 5-6	Theory Class
Saturday	Oct. 12	10:00-11:15	Level 1	Theory Class
		11:30-12:45	Level 2	Theory Class
Saturday	Oct. 19	10:00-11:15	Levels 3-4	Theory Class
		11:30-12:45	Levels 5-6	Theory Class
Sunday	Oct. 27	1:00-2:00	Beginning	Performance Class
		2:00-3:00	Intermediate	Performance Class
		3:00-4:00	Advanced	Performance Class
Saturday	Nov. 2	10:00-11:15	Level 1	Theory Class
		11:30-12:45	Level 2	Theory Class
Sunday	Nov. 10	1:00-2:00	Beginning	Performance Class
		2:00-3:00	Intermediate	Performance Class
		3:00-4:00	Advanced	Performance Class
Saturday	Nov. 16	10:00-11:15	Levels 3-4	Theory Class
		11:30-12:45	Levels 5-6	Theory Class
Saturday	Nov. 16	Ind. Times TBA		Fall Festival
Saturday	Nov. 23	10:00-11:15	Level 1	Theory Class
		11:30-12:45	Level 2	Theory Class
Saturday	Dec. 7	10:00-11:15	Levels 3-4	Theory Class
		11:30-12:45	Levels 5-6	Theory Class
Sunday	Dec. 8	1:00-3:00		Recital Rehearsal
Sunday	Dec. 15	7:00 p.m.		Recital

EXAMPLE 2

Mrs. Kathleen Jones•24 Main Street•Hometown, VA 12345
555-2222•mrsjones@hometown.net

September 2, 20--

COMING EVENTS CALENDAR FOR GROUP LESSONS TWO TIMES A MONTH

Please mark these dates on your calendar!
Save this copy for reference.

Tuesday	Sept. 3	7:00-8:00 p.m. 8:00-9:00 p.m.	Group 1 Group 2
Tuesday	Sept. 10	7:00-8:00 p.m. 8:00-9:00 p.m.	Group 3 Group 4 and above
Tuesday	Sept. 17	7:00-8:00 p.m. 8:00-9:00 p.m.	Group 1 Group 2
Tuesday	Sept. 24	7:00-8:00 p.m. 8:00-9:00 p.m.	Group 3 Group 4 and above
Tuesday	Oct. 1	7:00-8:00 p.m. 8:00-9:00 p.m.	Group 1 Group 2
Tuesday	Oct. 8	7:00-8:00 p.m. 8:00-9:00 p.m.	Group 3 Group 4 and above
Tuesday	Oct. 15	7:00-8:00 p.m. 8:00-9:00 p.m.	Group 1 Group 2
Tuesday	Oct. 22	7:00-8:00 p.m. 8:00-9:00 p.m.	Group 3 Group 4 and above
Tuesday	Oct. 29	7:00-8:00 p.m. 8:00-9:00 p.m.	Group 1 Group 2
Tuesday	Nov. 5	7:00-8:00 p.m. 8:00-9:00 p.m.	Group 3 Group 4 and above
Tuesday	Nov. 12	7:00-8:00 p.m. 8:00-9:00 p.m.	Group 1 Group 2
Tuesday	Nov. 19	7:00-8:00 p.m. 8:00-9:00 p.m.	Group 3 Group 4 and above
Tuesday	Nov. 26	7:00-8:00 p.m. 8:00-9:00 p.m.	Group 1 Group 2
Tuesday	Dec. 3	7:00-8:00 p.m. 8:00-9:00 p.m.	Group 3 Group 4 and above
Tuesday	Dec. 10	7:00-8:00 p.m. 8:00-9:00 p.m.	Group 1 Group 2
Tuesday	Dec. 17	7:00-8:00 p.m. 8:00-9:00 p.m.	Group 3 Group 4 and above

CHAPTER 5

SCHEDULING LESSONS

To establish a new schedule of lesson times, send out a letter similar to the example, with a copy of the hours you intend to teach and ask the parents to mark their first three choices on the schedule.

After all of the schedules have been returned, a master list can be made. Once all the students' three choices have been listed on a master list, lesson times can be chosen by process of elimination. Students can then be informed of their lesson time.

It is a good idea to give former students priority in choosing a lesson time, especially if last year's time is still their first choice. Let them know, however, that you cannot guarantee any time until the scheduling is completed.

Letter for Scheduling Example

Mrs. Kathleen Jones•24 Main Street•Hometown, VA 12345
555-2222•mrsjones@hometown.net

August 10, 20--

Dear Parents: (for adult students change to Dear Students:)

The new school year is just weeks away, and that means it is time to schedule lessons. Enclosed is a copy of the new policy sheet (please read it all) and a calendar of my teaching hours. Please mark no fewer than three options (#1, 2, 3) for a lesson time. If you want the same time as last year, please state that it was last year's time and I will try to give you priority, but there are no guarantees. If you have a flexible schedule, please mark as many options as possible. Every year I get 12 requests for 4:00 on Wednesdays, and that really makes scheduling hard!

The swap list has always been a big success. If you would like the option of swapping lesson times when you have a conflict, sign up for this list. I will publish the list of names, lesson times, and phone numbers so you can call other students to exchange a lesson time. Only those who sign up will be given a copy of the list.

Please return the enclosed schedule with your requests no later than August 20 if you would like to reserve a time.

Sincerely,

Kathleen Jones

encls.

Lesson Time Schedule Example

LESSON TIME SCHEDULE

Student's name ______________________ Phone ______________

Parents' daytime phones ______________________________

My first day of school this Fall is ______________________

My Spring Break is from ________________ to ________________

I do ____ do not ____ wish to be put on the Swap List.
_____ My first choice is last year's lesson time, which
was __________________.

Please mark 1st, 2nd, and 3rd choices (and other options if you wish).

MONDAY		TUESDAY	
1:45-2:30	________________	1:45-2:30	________________
2:30-3:15	________________	2:30-3:15	________________
3:15-4:00	________________	3:15-4:00	________________
4:00-4:45	________________	4:00-4:45	________________
7:00-7:45	________________	7:00-7:45	________________
7:45-8:30	________________	7:45-8:30	________________
8:30-9:15	________________	8:30-9:15	________________

Etc. for each teaching day.

Letter For Summer Lesson Time Example

Mrs. Kathleen Jones•24 Main Street•Hometown, VA 12345
555-2222•mrsjones@hometown.net

May 17, 20--

Dear Parents: (or Dear Students for adults)

Summer months are here at last! I'll be making a new schedule to accommodate summer students. I will be giving lessons all summer minus one week in August. On the enclosed Summer Lesson Time Schedule please mark your preferred lesson time. Be specific as to what your 1st, 2nd, and 3rd choices are. Mark as many possibilities as you can in case there are conflicts.

Students who are in town through the summer are expected to continue lessons. Otherwise, I cannot guarantee an opening for the Fall. Remember, summer is a very productive time for music, without any of the pressures of the school year.

The summer schedule is a little more flexible than the winter one. I will offer make-ups for pre-planned vacations—or we can prorate payments to accommodate lessons missed due to pre-planned trips. Make-ups will be given when a trip has been pre-arranged at least one week in advance, or for sickness when 24 hours notice is given. Please mark on the enclosed calendar any trips that you know of, and make a note about tentative dates.

Every August my schedule fills very quickly for the following term. I need to know now of any student, who, for any reason, will not be continuing in the Fall.

Remember that the new rates of $__________ for a 45-minute lesson and $__________ for a 60-minute lesson will go into effect June 1.

Sincerely,

Kathleen Jones
encls.

Summertime Lesson Schedule Example

SUMMERTIME LESSON SCHEDULE

Student's name________________ Phone________________

Parents' daytime phones________________

Please mark your 1st, 2nd, and 3rd choices and any other options.

	MONDAY	TUESDAY	WEDNESDAY	THURSDAY
10:00-10:45				
10:45-11:30				
11:30-12:15				
12:15-1:00				
1:00-1:45				
1:45-2:30				
2:30-3:15				
3:15-4:00				
4:00-4:45				
4:45-5:30				
7:00-7:45				
7:45-8:30				

Summer Vacation Schedule Example

SUMMER VACATION SCHEDULE

Student's name________________

Parent's daytime phones________________

My last day of school is________________

I do ____ do not ____ plan to take lessons in September.

Please mark any days you will be out of town this summer.

1	2	3	4	5	6	7
8	9	10	11	12	13	14
15	16	17	18	19	20	21
22	23	24	25	26	27	28
29	30	31				

(Calendars to be made for all summer months.)

CHAPTER 6

PROJECTING A PROFESSIONAL IMAGE

When dealing with parents and students, it is important to ALWAYS be at your professional best. Project a professional image and stick to your policies. If someone questions something that is stated in the policy sheet, do not justify, *clarify*.

It is important to dress in a business-like manner. Even though you may work at home, you are still working. Dress as if you were going to an office outside your home, or as if you were teaching in a school.

Introduce yourself to students and parents as "Miss, Ms., Mrs., Mr., or Dr.," whatever is appropriate. If you attempt to become friends with your clients right away it will be very difficult to maintain a professional relationship, and you will suffer for it when your friend asks a special favor "just this once."

If at all possible, keep your studio separate from the rooms used for personal use. This is the easiest way to receive a tax deduction for your studio space, and this arrangement will also help students to concentrate during their music lessons/classes.

Some key words and phrases to help present a professional image rather than a casual attitude include:

THIS	INSTEAD OF
Tuition	Lesson money
Theory class is at . . .	Could you make theory on . . .?
My records show . . .	Gee, I can't remember . . .
Mrs., etc.	Susie, John
The new policy is . . .	I'm really sorry and I hope you don't mind, but . . .
Due upon receipt	Can you pay me now?
Amount overdue	I really need the money you owe me from last month.

RECRUITING NEW STUDENTS

In order to attract new students, it is important to make yourself known in the community, generally and musically. For professional contacts, join the local chapter of a professional group such as the Music Teachers Association, the American Guild of Organists, the National Association of Teachers of Singing, or whatever is appropriate. More established teachers will learn of your availability. Joining is not enough, however; become active in the groups. The more established teachers will see this as a commitment to your profession. More importantly, you will become known and remembered. Teachers who only show up for one or two meetings will easily be forgotten. The more visible you are, the more likely you are to receive referrals from teachers who have an overflow of students.

In the general community, you may become more visible through schools, churches, synagogues, and libraries in your area. Establishing contacts is important, but being involved is crucial. Become active in the PTA, Scout troop, church or synagogue, women's or men's service clubs or other community groups. Let it be known that you are a music teacher and the word will spread.

Sending out flyers to neighborhoods and advertising in local newspapers is another method of getting known and is becoming increasingly popular.

PRESS RELEASE

A press release is a good method of free advertising. It can be used to "release" information about a recital of yours or your students, of workshops or conventions you have attended, of successes of present and past students, or other timely events. If a student is appearing in a local production, a press release is appropriate. Students love to see their names in print, and the attention given helps focus attention on the benefits of studying music. Remember neighborhood and school newspapers as well as organization newsletters.

CALL THE NEWSPAPER

Call the newspaper to confirm that the press release should be mailed to the Entertainment or Calendar Editor. If possible, get the name of that editor, or the name of whomever is to be sent the release, so the press release will not be delayed in getting to the correct person. For newspapers that have a section focused on grade and high school student achievements, you could also consider information about student recitals for that column.

Find out how far in advance the newspaper wishes to receive the release. This may vary from one to three weeks.

If the editor is available, and willing to discuss scheduling, you might both consider when the best time for the release to appear is. For instance, if the concert is on Friday evening and the weekly calendar of events appears on Fridays only, do you want it to appear on the day of your concert or the week before? If you want it to appear both times, do you need to send two separate releases?

CONTENTS OF THE PRESS RELEASE

Include the basics. Avoid any "hype" about what a wonderful program this will be. The newspaper will avoid any such endorsements. Instead, give the important facts.

Who:	The name of the person or group performing.
What:	The instrument(s) being played; the music on the program.
Where:	The building, street address, town; neighborhood if it applies.
When:	The date and time.
Fee:	Information about costs, donations, or free.
Contact person:	Name and daytime phone number of someone who can answer questions from the editor should anything need clarification.
Why:	Do not include the answer to this unless, for instance, the concert is a benefit. You might include some information about the background or training of the musician(s), but do not be surprised if it is not included.

FORMAT OF THE RELEASE

The release should be no longer than three or four paragraphs, double-spaced with wide margins. (Examples of press releases are given.)

Notice the format used in the newspaper and write as closely to that format as possible. When appropriate and available, send a black and white glossy photograph—not a snapshot.

FOLLOW-UP

This is an area you might wish to investigate when you first call to confirm the editor's name. Ask if you could call several days after sending the press release to verify that it arrived. Be careful of taking too much of the editor's time on the phone—you do want "good handling" this time as well as the next. Editors are often working with very tight schedules.

Press Release Example #1

Mrs. Kathleen Jones•24 Main Street•Hometown, VA 12345
555-2222•mrsjones@hometown.net

May 10, 20--

PRESS RELEASE
for publication between May 20 and May 28.

Contact: Kathleen Jones, 555-2222 between 9-2.

WHO: Students, ranging in age from 4-13, of Kathleen Jones.

WHAT: Violin recital

WHERE: Mayberry Community Center, 217 Main Street

WHEN: Saturday, May 28, 2 p.m.

ADMISSION: Free

The violin students of Kathleen Jones will give a recital on Saturday, May 28 at 2:00 p.m. Mayberry resident Jones has been a teacher in the area for 15 years and her students have been active in many local recitals, festivals, and competitions. The recital will be held at the Mayberry Community Center at 217 Main Street in Mayberry. Admission is free and refreshments will be served after the recital.

Press Release Example #2

Mrs. Kathleen Jones•24 Main Street•Hometown, VA 12345
555-2222•mrsjones@hometown.net

January 5, 20--

PRESS RELEASE
for publication between January 17 and 23

Contact: Kathleen Jones, 555-2222 between 9-2.

WHO: Kathleen Jones and Stephanie James

WHAT: Violin/Piano Recital

WHERE: W.J. Thompson Library, 2100 Maple Drive, Mayberry

WHEN: Sunday, January 23, 7 p.m.

ADMISSION: $10

Violinist Kathleen Jones and pianist Stephanie James will be performing a recital at the W.J. Thompson Library, 2100 Maple Drive, Mayberry, on Sunday January 23, at 7:00 p.m. Mayberry resident Jones is a member of the Mayberry Chamber Orchestra and the Sidney Quartet and teaches students of all ages. James, a piano teacher in Mayberry, is also organist at the Third Congregational Church. The program will include music by Bach, Ravel, and Bartók. Admission is $10.00; tickets may be purchased at the door. Call the library at 555-7342 for more information.

Press Release Example #3

Mrs. Kathleen Jones•24 Main Street•Hometown, VA 12345
555-2222•mrsjones@hometown.net

July 10, 20--

PRESS RELEASE
for immediate release through July 30, 20--

For information: Kathleen Jones, 555-2222 between 9-2.

WHO: Area brass bands

WHAT: Mayberry Brass Band Festival

WHERE: W.J. Thompson Library Lawn, 2100 Maple Drive, Mayberry

WHEN: Wednesday, July 30, 7:30 p.m.

ADMISSION: Free

The Fairfax County Recreation Department and the Mayberry Music Teachers Association will present the Mayberry Brass Band Festival on Wednesday July 30, 20-- at 7:30 p.m. on the lawn of the W.J. Thompson Library, 2100 Maple Drive, Mayberry. Brass bands from Mayberry and three surrounding counties will be performing the music of American composers.

The concert is free and open to the public. For comfort, bring a chair or blanket to sit on. For additional information call the Fairfax County Recreation Department at 555-4232 or 555-0522.

CHAPTER 7

BUSINESS & FINANCIAL PRACTICES

BOOKKEEPING & BUDGETING

When budgeting for the coming year, it is imperative to have an accurate record of expenses and income for the current year. You can achieve this by keeping a monthly record of expenses, and from that record you will better know how to judge for next year. Accurate record keeping is essential to running any business.

It is easy to establish good bookkeeping procedures. Buy a music record book, or a general bookkeeping book. In a general one, one page can be used to record monthly expenses, another to record student payments (examples are given for both). The minute you receive a check, record it in the book under that student's name for that month. Another page can be used to record student attendance. When a student arrives, record the date. If they do not come, and it is an unexcused absence, record a "U" where the date would normally be recorded. If it is an excused absence, leave that entry blank until that lesson is made up, and then record the date on which it was made up. If there is no scheduled lesson that week, Columbus Day for example, record a "/" in place of a date or a "U."

	9/1	9/8	9/15	9/22	9/29	10/6	10/13
Jeff Price	9/1	9/8	U	9/22		10/6	/
Michelle Stillwell	9/1		9/15	9/22	9/29	U	/
(etc.)							

Monthly Payment Schedule Example

MONTHLY PAYMENT SCHEDULE

	Sept.	Oct.	Nov.	Dec.	Jan.	Feb.	Mar.	Apr.	May	June	July	Aug.
ALLEN, JASON 586-5103 6943 Prairie, Alexandria 22305												
BURCKHALTER, DAVID 546-8169 208 N. Reed, Alex. 22305												
JAMES, MARCIA 546-1332 9108 Bryant Lane #21A, Alex. 22310												
LEE, GINA 283-5136 1312 Sunset Lane, Alex. 22333												
PARSONS, BARBARA 544-7768 1203 N. Rector, Alex. 22345												
(etc.)												

ITEMS TO BUDGET

This list is not meant to be comprehensive, but it is a good starting point when developing a budget.

HOME

Rent or mortgage
Food/household goods
Telephone
Electricity
Gas
Water
Repairs
Insurance

CAR/TRANSPORTATION

Gas/oil
Maintenance
Insurance
Car registration fee*
Personal property tax*
Car loan
Bus/subway/taxi
Parking

TAXES

Federal*
State*
Property*
Tax preparation

MEDICAL/HEALTH

Prescriptions
Health insurance
Medical costs after insurance
Dental

MISCELLANEOUS

Life insurance
Entertainment
Savings
Credit cards
Other ____________

BUSINESS/MUSIC

Dues/publications*
Music
Concert tickets
Instrument maintenance, repair, tuning
Machine repairs (stereos, computers)
Music lessons
Conventions, workshop fees
Studio rental
Business license*
Office supplies/postage
Secretarial fees
Copying/printing
Studio maintenance
Insurance for studio/instruments/computer/studio furnishings
Instrument rental
Entertainment (student party, lunch meeting with colleagues)/public relations
Other ____________

*Quarterly or yearly expenses

Monthly Expenses Chart Example

MONTHLY EXPENSES CHART

	Sept.	Oct.	Nov.	Dec.	Jan.	Feb.	Mar.	Apr.	May	June	July	Aug.
Mortgage/rent												
Electricity												
Gas heat												
Water												
Phone												
Office supplies/postage												
Copying/printing												
Business dues/publications												
Music books												
Instrument maintenance												
Convention/workshop fees												
Concert tickets												
Car payments												
Car maintenance												
Gasoline/oil												
Car insurance												
Health insurance												
Prescriptions												
Dental												
Business license												
IRS quarterly payments												
State tax quarterly												
Personal property tax												
Tax preparation												

(etc.)

INCOME TAX DEDUCTIONS FOR TEACHER/ MUSICIAN

Tax laws change from year to year and differ from state to state. It is best to check with a tax consultant if there are questions, especially after a move to another state. The following list contains examples of *possible* tax deductions for the independent music teacher. Check with the IRS or an accountant to obtain a list of what is deductible in your specific case.

There are practices you must develop if you expect to receive tax deductions for your business. Most importantly, *keep accurate records*. The "burden of proof" is on you. Keep receipts to ALL music functions attended (ticket stubs, charge receipts, etc.). Keep a mileage log for all business-related mileage (to concerts, to buy music, to conventions or recitals, etc.). Keep receipts for all studio-related expenses (furniture, insurance, music, instrument and machine maintenance, etc.).

Obtain a copy of the tax form used for self-employed individuals. Take note of the categories listed. Many of the deductions allowed for your studio will be categorized under "Other." Divide these specialized "Other" expenses into sub-categories and keep your records according to the sub-categories. General business expenses (such as mileage) will appear on the tax form.

Keep your receipts organized. You may file them by category in a notebook, in an expanding file, or in individual file folders in a file cabinet. When you file your receipt, be sure to note *how* it relates to your business. Again, it is important to keep your records organized in order to avoid an end-of-the-year panic, and to be sure that you have received tax credit for all eligible expenses.

Your studio is deductible as a "home office" if that room, or that portion of a room, is used solely for the purpose of your business. If your studio takes up 20% of the liveable space in your home (attic and basement storage not included), then 20% of your household insurance, utility bills, and other bills relating to the entire house may be used as a deduction.

Tax laws can be very confusing. Even though the cost of an accountant seems like a big expense, it is well worth it. An accountant is invaluable in helping to establish proper bookkeeping procedures and outlining allowable deductions, especially for your first year of itemizing. Even with an accountant, you still need to keep your own records and receipts.

The following information was prepared by Kay Bjelland, for the Independent Music Teacher Forum, South Central Division of MTNA.

GROSS INCOME

Includes amounts from lessons, recitals, lectures, etc.

DEDUCTIONS

1. Music, records, tapes, etc.—includes music purchased for studio.
2. Advertising.
3. Bank service charges.
4. Office supplies—statements, envelopes, adding machine tape, pencils, pens, erasers, paper clips, etc.
5. Postage for statements, Christmas cards for music associates, various cards and notices mailed to students, etc.
6. Dues and subscriptions: magazines, organization/ professional dues and assessments, etc.
7. Insurance: pro-rate part of residence for studio, instruments, and studio furnishings.
8. Utilities: pro-rate part of residential charges for studio.
9. Telephone: include business long-distance calls.
10. Piano and organ tuning.
11. Repairs to equipment, furniture, air conditioning, heating, plumbing, etc.
12. Teaching supplies: teaching aids, chalk, erasers, blackboard, pencils and pens, tissues, toilet tissue if studio is in residence.
13. Studio rental if any; instrument rental.
14. Taxes: pro-rate part of residence for studio, also state sales tax on equipment.
15. Auto expense: mileage to attend meetings, purchase music, attend seminars, rehearsals, visit pupils, etc.
16. Parking expenses.

17. Payments to substitute or associate teachers.
18. Recital expenses: hall rental, programs, decorations, refreshments, etc.
19. Entertainment and public relations: club meetings; Christmas cards and gifts to students; other gifts—graduation, birthday, illness, parents' parties, etc.; cold drinks, etc. for students; luncheons and dinners for out-of-town associates; local entertainment.
20. Music awards.
21. Travel expense: hotels, meals, tips, etc., for conventions and meetings.
22. Teacher seminars, including books and supplies and any other related expense.
23. Depreciation on studio, instruments, music library, record player, tape recorder, computer, studio furnishings, air conditioner, etc.
24. Christmas tree and decorations for studio; other seasonal decorations throughout the year.

ZONING LAWS

In most cities and counties there are laws that apply to home businesses, and thus to the independent music teacher. These laws may restrict how many students are allowed in the studio at one time, how many individual lessons may be taught in a day, the amount of sound that can be generated from a home business, or the effect that business can have on local parking. Often, a letter of approval from the zoning office or an Occupancy Permit is needed before a business license will be granted. The purpose of such a letter is to state that the zoning laws have been read and agreed upon before the business license has been granted. The purpose of the zoning laws as they apply to music studios is to insure that independent studios in residential neighborhoods do not become large enough to be called music schools, and do not disrupt the neighborhood by excess traffic, activity, or noise.

BUSINESS LICENSES

A business license is usually required to legally run a private studio in the home. In rare cases, if income is under a certain level, a business license is not required. There is a minimum fee for teachers who earn up to a certain amount of income per year. As income rises above that set amount (which varies by county), the fee for the business license rises and is prorated. It is illegal to operate a business without a license when one is required. When such a case arises, there is a penalty, based on the gross receipts of past years, usually the last three years plus the current year.

TANGIBLE BUSINESS TAX

Any tangible item that is declared a deduction on the federal income tax forms is subject to a tangible business tax. Examples of such items are instruments, music cabinets, recording equipment, computer, etc. This tax is put in action once a teacher acquires a business license. If a teacher is late in receiving that license, and must pay a penalty for past years, he will also have to pay past tangible business taxes.

CHAPTER 8

STUDIO POLICY SURVEY

Do you wonder if you are undercharging? Are you offering make-up lessons for any, or all, reasons when most teachers in your area are not? Do you dislike half-hour lessons, yet feel you have to teach them because everyone else does? Are you offering enough services compared to other teachers? Do you know what is a reasonable fee for lessons in your area?

We often learn best from each other. Shared information on policies can help music teachers to better understand the rates and business practices currently in use in their area. You can obtain this information by speaking with area teachers, or consulting with the officers of a local professional organization.

Another, perhaps more reliable, method of gaining insight into the practices of area music teachers is to conduct a studio policy survey. By sharing information with each other, we can learn of ways other teachers simplify the logistics of teaching. By discovering the average hourly rate for our area, for example, we may discover that our own rate is too low. We may feel we must always offer make-ups or we will lose students. A survey may show that the majority of teachers offer make-ups only rarely. We may discover that very few teachers offer half-hour lessons, and that we need not feel obligated to do so. Perhaps most teachers offer theory classes, and you should also in order to remain competitive.

The sample questionnaire included on the following pages will demonstrate the kind of information which might be useful. If a local teachers' group wished to conduct a survey, it could be distributed at a meeting or mailed to the members. The members could answer the questions anonymously and mail the completed forms to a designated member. The member who agrees to tally the results could then average the answers, use percentages, or provide summaries of the answers to best represent the policies of the responding teachers. For example:

Number of teachers responding:	60
Average years teaching experience:	21
What levels do you teach?	
Beginning to intermediate	15
Intermediate to advance	10
All levels	35

If percentages are preferred, the answers might be given in the following manner:

What levels do you teach?	
Beginning to intermediate	25%
Intermediate to advanced	16%
All levels	58%

What do you see as the biggest drawback or problem in running your business?

Hours—either too long or inconvenient	25%
Paperwork/extra work	16%
Make-ups/scheduling	8%
Teaching in home	8%
Inadequate salary	5%

MUSIC TEACHERS' STUDIO POLICY QUESTIONNAIRE

from A Business Guide for the Music Teacher

by Beth Gigante

What instruments/subjects do you teach?__________
How many students do you teach (on the average)?__________
What levels do you teach? beginning intermediate advanced all
How many years teaching experience do you have?__________
What music organizations do you belong to?__________
What is your educational background? (Include major and minor of any degree.)__________

What length lesson do you normally teach?__________
What length lesson do you prefer?__________
What services do you provide for students other than a weekly lesson, and how often?
Give any extra information.__________

____ Workshops
____ Theory classes
____ Recitals
____ Group lessons
____ Competitions
____ Book supplies
____ Other (describe)__________

How do you bill?
____ Monthly (beginning or ending?)
____ Weekly
____ Semester (explain)
____ Other (describe)__________
What tuition do you charge for students taking 60-minute lessons? (Even if you do not give 60-minute lessons, please compute this fee so an average may be reached.)__________
If appropriate, what do you charge for 60-minute group lessons?__________
How do you bill for books, supplies, fees?__________

Do you give discounts for families?__________
Do you interview prospective students before accepting them?__________
On the average, how often do your rates increase?__________
What is your financial policy concerning a dropping student?__________

Do you have a written policy sheet?__________
What is your policy concerning make-up lessons?__________

****

How do you feel about how much you earn?

If you could charge more, what would you charge?

What do you see as the biggest drawback or problem in running your business?

How do you feel about your make-up policy?

How would you change your make-up policy?

If you were to set up an ideal policy and business, what would it include?

Are you aware of the zoning laws in your area?

Do you have a Business License?